This book belongs to:

_____

When Daddy Goes Away

Marie Hinkle

Illustrated by
Katie Dwyer

5 Sail Publishing
Jacksonville, Florida

Copyright © 2020 Marie Hinkle

All rights reserved. No part of this book may be reproduced, stored in a retrieval system, or transmitted in any form or by any means, electronic, mechanical, photocopying, recording, or otherwise, without written permission from the publisher 5 Sail Publishing, 14286 Beach Blvd., Ste. 19-277, Jacksonville, FL 32250, or through the publisher's website, www.5SailPublishing.com.

Book and cover design by Sagaponack Books & Design

ISBNs:
978-1-7341248-3-5 (softcover)
978-1-7341248-4-2 (hardcover)
978-1-7341248-5-9 (e-book)

Library of Congress Control Number: 2020920389

Summary: A young child expresses her feelings and shows how her daily routines change when her father is deployed.

JUV013060 Juvenile Fiction / Family / Parents
JUV039050 Juvenile Fiction / Social Themes / Emotions & Feelings
JUV015010 Juvenile Fiction / Health & Daily Living / Daily Activities
JUV039140 Juvenile Fiction / Social Themes / Self-Esteem & Self-Reliance

5 Sail Publishing
Jacksonville, Florida

Printed and bound in the United States of America
First Edition

This book is dedicated to my family and all the military families affected by a deployment. My dad was in the military, as well as my husband. I truly understand what that life is like and I completely appreciate all of their sacrifices. It takes a tremendous amount of strength to endure those hardships. Thank you for all you do for our country. This book is for you.

*I may not always be with you
But when we're far apart
Remember you will be with me
Right inside my heart.*

—Marc Wambolt

When Daddy Goes Away

When Daddy goes away,
I am Mommy's big helper.
I help wash and fold the laundry.

I make my bed each day and get dressed.

I even help watch my brother. I am really good at making him laugh, with my funny faces.

He loves when I play with him.

When Daddy goes away, I get to watch a movie in Mommy's bed. We cuddle and eat popcorn.

When Daddy goes away,
I help Mommy grocery shop.
They have a cart just for me.

When Daddy goes away,
we go on a shopping spree.
Shh … don't tell Daddy.

When Daddy goes away,
I miss him very much.

We talk on the phone and I see him through the computer. I even get to read to him.

I listen to the teacher and do my best at school.

Mommy tells me Daddy is working for our family. He is protecting our country.

I draw him pictures and write him notes. I send them in the mail.

Mommy says Daddy loves to get something special in the mail.

When he comes home,
we are going to swing,
play tag in the grass,
and swim in the pool.

At night, we will read books together.

I made a "Welcome home" sign for when he comes back. I have a pretty dress to wear.

We count down the days with chocolate candies.
I can't wait until Daddy is home.

Daddy is strong and smart. I want him to know that I think he is the best.

In the meantime, when Daddy goes away, I am Mommy's big helper.

Deployment Suggestions

1. **Countdown:** (a) Make a paper chain, hang it, and let your child rip off one link for each day. (b) Fill a jar with small objects for your child to take out, one each day. This gives children a visual for how many days there are before their loved one returns.

2. **Book of memories:** Put together a scrapbook with your child, to send to your loved one or share with them when they return.

3. **Story time:** Record favorite bedtime stories read by your loved one—before deployment. Children can listen to a story each night while following along in the book.

4. **Love packages:** Help your child assemble packages filled with letters, drawings, photographs, special treats, and treasures to ship to their loved one.

5. **Calls and chats:** Set up a special time for your children to call or video chat with their loved one. Share experiences from the day, read, or do homework together.

6. **Staying close:** Create plush toys, blankets, and shirts made with photographs of your loved one, for your child to wear or hold close.

Make your own list:

1.

2.

3.

ABOUT THE AUTHOR

Marie Hinkle is a seasoned educator who has had the opportunity to teach in several schools across the United States. This is her second published children's book. The first one is titled *Unique and Me*. Mrs. Hinkle is passionate about reading and empowering children. She lives in Florida with her husband, three kids, one cat, one dog, and a turtle. Her family has inspired her to write several books. In her free time, she loves to travel and spend time with her family at the beach.

Learn more about Marie at 5sailpublishing.com.

ABOUT THE ILLUSTRATOR

Katie Dwyer fell in love with art at a young age and could often be found drawing pictures and pretending the day away. She began her career as a children's book illustrator and hasn't looked back. She loves eating tacos and drinking iced matcha lattes. Her home, in California, is shared with her husband and three little wildlings.

www.ingramcontent.com/pod-product-compliance
Lightning Source LLC
Chambersburg PA
CBHW042029100526
44587CB00029B/4348